Meditative as the monastery he inhabited in the writing of this b... *Shield the Joyous* contemplates not only the loss of a brother through addiction but the search for deeper understanding. These poems mourn. They engage in magical thinking, exuding wonderment toward death. They traverse the gulf of detachment to find solace and wisdom in the earth. Eventually the poet is "led ... to the I, to that inner self to which [he'd] been working [his] way toward all along."
—**Joseph O. Legaspi**, cofounder of *Kundiman*, and author of *Threshold*

Shield the Joyous is a work of great wonderment and love, amidst "the ghostly whirl" of the author's own grief and loss. His baby brother has died of addiction and there is much to think about — so into the deep quiet of a monastery he goes, where the gloom and majesty of memory and trouble surge and mix alongside the Hudson River and the swirl is able to illuminate, settle, calm. "I was elsewhere \ when my brother died" — but the writer is fully present now, to honor his sibling with rich care and tender thinking and writing that will help anyone who has ever lost anyone, now and forever, amen.
—**Naomi Shihab Nye**, the Young People's Poet Laureate, and author or editor of over 30 volumes, most recently *The Tiny Journalist*

Shield the Joyous is a powerful memoir of a man's journey in coming to terms with his brother's drug addiction and subsequent death. It is a deeply spiritual book, conceived in a monastery where the author goes on retreats to recover from loss and save himself. It is also a survival guide, lifting us all out of despair. In the sublime manner of W. H. Auden, Shade builds his work on the canonical hours, beautifully combining prose and poetry to express intense emotion.
—**Grace Schulman**, author most recently *Without a Claim*

Shield the Joyous

Christopher X. Shade

Paloma Press, 2020

ISBN 978-1-7323025-9-4

Library of Congress Control Number: 2020930703

Cover Image by Christopher X. Shade

Author Photograph by Beowulf Sheehan

Book Design by C. Sophia Ibardaloza

Also by Christopher X. Shade
The Good Mother of Marseille

PALOMA PRESS
San Mateo & Morgan Hill, California
Publishing Poetry+Prose since 2016
www.palomapress.net

in memory of Matthew Stephen Misko, 1984-2017

And the budded peaks of the wood are bow'd,
Caught and cuff'd by the gale
—**Lord Alfred Tennyson**, *Maud VI.1.*

There is an evening coming in
Across the fields, one never seen before,
That lights no lamps.
—**Philip Larkin**, *Going*

CONTENTS

PREFACE

My baby brother was found nonresponsive on Christmas day in 2017, and he died that night. He suffered the disease of addiction. He lived a rural life in Alabama, while my life in New York City may as well have been happening on another planet in our solar system. He and I lived in very different places, and, really, at different times. We were not close in age. And, we were. Our lives are complicated; the lines on family trees, our blood lines, the lines by which we are connected to one another, all of us. But despite this, despite distance and differences, there's no reason for any of us to grow apart from one another.

My baby brother died of acute liver failure secondary to alcoholic liver disease. He died of alcoholic cirrhosis. He had a systemic infection, septicemia. In the ambulance on the way to the hospital, he had a heart attack. They kept him breathing, but by the time they got him to the hospital, he was already gone.

The loss hit me hard. And, it was familiar. I'd heard about this from so many people—isn't loss of loved ones to addiction like a raging forest fire, one we suggest could never happen at our home? Until suddenly it does.

I went on a series of retreats to a monastery on the Hudson River in New York, where I wrote this book. Poetry, the form, gave me enough detachment from the pain to produce this book which I intended to be vivid in its specificity while its characters are more archetypal than not; it is a work that helped me to grapple to understand the distance that grows between loved ones when there's addiction, to better understand myself.

The structure is an horarium, which is a schedule of prayers at the monastery. The title is a line from the prayers at Compline, at the conclusion of the day. After Compline, there is silence until the next morning after breakfast. And it means a lot to me, this phrase, to shield the joyous. Because my baby brother was a joyful child. If only I had known to, or thought to, shield him.

C. X. Shade, "Chris"
March 2019
New York City

MATINS

THE FIRST THING I said this morning
was thank you.   §

THE TRAIN WHISTLE from across the Hudson
does not shriek, it harrumphs.   §

MARY AND JOSEPH NOTICED
that Jesus had to pull things closer to see them.
And so it went that in his fifth year Jesus was given glasses.
They were like the ones I had as a boy,
they were enormous on his face,
and no one told him how ridiculous he looked.
This was how it was and is and always will be.
And a little time passed, the time of children,
the playtime that I did not know would mean so much,
climbing trees, wandering dry creek beds.
He was able to distinguish
the donkey at pasture from the dog,
and trees, the olive from the almond.
And so it came to pass that his vision got worse,
but this wasn't as important as
food on the table, and shoes, and so as he grew
he wore the glasses but could not see true.
Time and again as prophesied
he could not read transit signs
and got turned around in New York City.
He missed buses.
He missed appearances
at peace rallies
and birthdays at Rosa Mexicano.
But who better knew,
who better than this visionary,
that to fall out of touch
is to fall into peril?
The subway brought him
from way out in Queens
to SoHo TriBeCa NoLita and NoHo
where I've seen him, yes there,
among shoppers who golf
and own beach homes.
I've seen him
at the top of subway station stairs
like a pickpocket

of passports and souls,
watching from behind
enormous glasses
the blur of all peoples
passersby. §

A BUG BOUNCES OFF A LEAF

—but where is it now? It is shaken. It is lost. It drifts over one lawn, then over another lawn. It tumbles in a wind gust and then recovers its ballast. It peers in the windows of houses. Its antennae receive faint transmissions that are incomprehensible. Curious—it is lost! In the near distance, it swears that it can hear bug grownups working, it hears bug children playing. How to find them? Dread soaks down into its body. Is this a familiar flower? Yes! Or, is it not? What about this one? No, it's not familiar after all…and really for a long time in its life all flowers have seemed the same. Hasn't it, in its diseases of addiction, desired detachment. It follows another bug as far as it can—but no, this is its own reflection on a pond. Its mother, long gone, grabbed by a spider, taken, wrapped. The bug will never forget diving away, afraid— leaving its mother behind! Such guilt the bug feels! Its father, taken in the beak of a swooping black bird. Who's left to love the bug, anyway? But its separation remains insufferable. As if abandoned, as if discarded. Though no one is to blame but itself, because the bug is its wanderings. It inhabits the vacuity of its lush, leafing world. It embodies a desperate pursuit of nowhere, finally.   §

THE TRAIN'S ARCHETYPE
is the chariot.
The Hudson towboat's archetype
is the rowboat
and the ferry.
The poor soul who suffers
winter on a towboat
to push a barge
wakes up to fog
and engine drone,
pulls on boots
and leaves warm bunk
for cold wet metal,
with a cargo
of blue bridge girders,
road salt, or crude.
Above deck,
a lamp makes
a cotton ball of fog.
And this soul
too vivid for archetype
is so grateful
for the hot coffee
when it's ready.   §

3 BY 3
it's a game
of dots on paper
9 dots in all
plus the line,
the line we draw
without lifting the pencil
to begin at one
and join the others
the assumptions
that allowed me
to neglect concerns
despite the years passing
with no news of you.

The first line on paper
has to be true.
No news from you:
the diminishing circle,
the first diagnostic
of a life in peril,
as David Whyte suggests.

It's never clear
until the second line
that the dot game
has gone to shit.

I'm left outside the box
alone, corded with curiosity,
and sorrowful uncertainty,
at this monastery
on a frozen Hudson
and you curl up
in ash
at the monastery in Alabama
they say the 9 dot game

may be solved
on a sphere, like our planet,
the dots in one place,
if only we were,
under the blush and scarlet
of poplars and hickories,
and pines,
together.   §

WHERE I'M FROM
Alabama
magnolia grandiflora
lenten rose
oak leaf hydrangea
Memphis
camellia, camellia, camellia
my granny, Camille,
who smoked Camel cigarettes
Pensacola
grandma's azaleas
and grandpa's sago palms.   §

I'M A DUCK ON A POND.

I kick underwater. Sometimes when there are no ripples I look at myself and I do have wisdom enough to wonder at what I see, when what I see is the reflection of me, the shimmering sheen of my green, and I wonder at how I do not know me.

As for me, the pond, I don't know much about ducks except they get hunted, shot, and killed in these bottomlands of North Alabama. Men in waders with shotguns, usually in or out of an outboard motor boat that is the color of the tall grass and ferns. While a pond like me is not a pond, it's fed from somewhere, it's feeding somewhere else, it's all tributary, it's all the same in this Alabama portion of the Tennessee Valley. A boat disturbs me but not for long. Really it leaves no trace. Water spiders tickle me. A dragonfly follows my curves. Sunlight graces me. I toss a frog out into the grass and it hops back, it plops belly first into me.

I'm the tall grass the men are trying to see over. I want to be taller but I'm only what I am. I know what the duck does not know is on the other side of me, and I know what the men do not know is on the other side of me. I'm a barrier to men's dreams. I'm in the way but I'm not built to do anything about it. I'm rooted. Under the water, my roots grip the soft clay.

In these parts, I'm the soil under the water and the same soil that's up under the boat the men have pulled out of the water. I'm the red clay and sandstone and dark loam. I hold everything down and I let things live as they choose to live and when a thing dies the men come to me with shovels. Shotgun shells fall to me. When a duck is shot, the duck falls to me and one man walks across me to get it. When he can't find his kill then the other men join him to search through the tall grass, and they walk all around and spit on me and push sticks into me and leave their boot prints.

The men stink, and I shift and swirl and carry their stench through tall grass and over water and further out into the pine woods. On my signal, a number of good living things flee. But

I cannot stop a shotgun's discharge. It goes right through the ghostly whirl of me. I am the air in which all things exist and in which all things suffer. I witness and I have held the space for all of histories. I fill the feathers and full the wings of a duck lifting off from a pond. I am the wind. And when the shotgun explodes and the duck collapses upon itself and falls tumbling through me, when this happens I die, too. I am the dead calm.   §

IS A YOUNGER BROTHER
an echo
and is a half brother
how much quieter
an echo
or how much louder
an echo
over how much less time
of a rosary slipping
to the next bead
of a penitent in a pew.
All of the sounds, words we said,
words you said, all the way back to ancient times,
with pizza dough flung in the air,
biology lectures you heard,
sand dollars you found wailing
on Perdido Beach
alone,
with ringing telephones
I never answered,
echoes
kick in my damn gut.   §

MY RICE KRISPIES tell me that every night and morning are a death and resurrection.

No one else here at breakfast in the monastery dining room is talking. We are subject to The Great Silence. Same as the family of white-tailed deer grazing the grassy expanse between the monastery and the Hudson. Their rice krispies of winter grass tell them that there are deaths with a lowercase d and deaths with a capital D. This morning I'm furious, reading that in 1970 Celan leaped into the Seine, and I'm furious that my baby brother was lost to pills and booze on Christmas Day. When we lose poets, we lose language. When we lose the young, we lose the future. I'm ashamed; I am of no use. Of what use am I? Of what use is anger? The tree toad's rice krispies of grub and spiders tell it that upon resurrection there is no greater disaster than to be immersed in unreality, as Thomas Merton wrote, for we are nourished by our vital relations with realities. Death, the finch is told by its rice krispies of reed grass seed, is a complete gift of ourselves. Among what I can grasp of the incomprehensibility of such things, my rice krispies are in milk from New Britain, Connecticut, what they say is the bovine divine.   §

TORN PAPERS
of monastery verse
are garbled communications
from the living to the dead
on the windowsill and the desk
soon to be gathered up
and thrown out.
Today's fog on the Hudson
has the ragged edge of torn paper,
and so do treetops on the fog
and gray sky on the trees.
I ache inside like this:
ripped to pieces, and ashen.
I ought to be thrown out.
I can't see the rain.
I see its haze,
I see dead children
running on winter grass
and I feel the rain on my face.
Its taps are forlorn
while a somewhere bird
chirps to it, in minor key.
In Aesop's fable,
the blue jay
and the peacock, we
learned who we were.
This somewhere bird
whose measures mete grief
is neither jay nor finely feathered.
It's a common brown and
delicate bird, hardly
more than a fluff of feathers,
so small, and so slight.
If I hadn't known you
when you were a joyful child,
red-haired and smiling,
wide-eyed with wonder,

if I hadn't known you,
would I have chosen you
to call brother?
I don't know, what an impossible
question, and the shame is unbearable.
The most painful part
is, without hesitation,
you would've said
you would've chosen me.
Today the trumpet of train whistle
as John wrote in Revelations
and from under this:
the many waters
lapping at this side of things,
at this shore of stones,
dead wood, and moss.   §

BOARD GAMES WHEN IT RAINED
all of us kids wanted
to play Risk again,
the world at war,
but you wanted to play
Candyland. Such a baby,
you were the baby
of the family.
When we wanted
Monopoly's Oriental
Avenues, all you wanted
was Candy Cane Forest
and Gumdrop Mountain.
We'd even settle for Life—
though it was shit, this game,
with its spinning wheel,
its families in convertibles
and days of reckoning—
but you were in protest,
for Candyland had no gloom,
no bankruptcy, no failure.
It wasn't until you became
a pill head
along the winding roads
we left you to wander,
around corners
and over bridges,
and a drunk, where we left you
feeling lost, when it
occurred to me
as it does saints, priests,
shrinks, and football
coaches, those with sight,
that I should've seen it coming.
I should've known
that I would lose you

to a Candyland
of colored pills.   §

WHILE YOU REST, I take a turn on the red bike
where pines pillar the black dirt.
The woods have been cleared
by brushfire, disease and helmeted ants.

The boy on the bicycle of uncertainty
stands on the pedal to throw the brake,
and he skids. He carves, cleaving earwigs
from spindly fish-skeleton beetles
fat fungus gnats from sod webworms
worms! so many worms!
in the kickup of dirt and stones.
When his slide is sluggish
he leans back to lift the wheel.
He's in heaven.
He hits a little hill and leaps.
He hits a hill and leaps
further out into the yawns, alone.

The thrill of the safe landing.
He expects to land safe
despite his fragility
and all that would kill him
the worn brake pads
the skipping chain a crooked frame
frayed cables and rust
and loose bolts on the stem.
How to throw the boy from the bike?
Brush diseased dust from his clothes
get him inside, wash his hands of this.   §

DIURNUM

I LEFT THE MONASTERY'S GUESTHOUSE in the bracing cold wind.

I followed the perimeter of the yard, past the garden where crocuses were blooming, and daffodils were emerging, and fingers of hyacinth stood up from the earth, and I went past the statue of Saint Stefan, a tall bearded man. It was my name for him, this statue who might be any saint, for what is a name, after all? And from the statue I went onward along the perimeter of the yard in a giant letter C down to the wooded paths that led to the water, the Hudson. Paths, I followed, this path, and that path. A letter H of paths, and there was a red birdhouse nailed onto a tree at the paths where they crossed. But it was not a birdhouse. It was a wood thing in the shape of a house painted red, the letter R of red, with a figure inside of it. The figure was Christ, solemn, with eyes looking back at me, and it led me to the I, to that inner self to which I'd been working my way toward all along.   §

THE LAWNMOWER
was not easy for me—
you may remember
me with the lawnmower.
I remember you, out in the yard
chewing a stalk of bluegrass,
seed head at the other end,
how to describe how you
sat for hours like that
a red-haired baby Buddha
how could I have known then
that you'd be a lost Buddha
who desires detachment
an addict
when what mattered to me
was getting the hell through high school
and shit for pay jobs
what mattered to me
was getting in my shit car,
slamming doors,
throwing the car into gear
I kept the windows up
until the house was out of sight
what mattered to me
was having been whipped
slapped told was shit stupid
my boyhood stolen from me
by your father
and then mowing the goddamn grass
in our searing Alabama heat
bluegrass and crab and clover
among prickly dandelions
the cupped hands of broadleaf plantain
grassburs
the wounds of wild strawberry
and I did, just that,
for as long as I could.

Your father was not mine
but still, my red-haired Buddha brother,
the complicated lines by
which we are among one another.
The simple lines
like a stalk of bluegrass
by which we love.　§

ALONE, in the cold day
with my knees at my chest
my boots up on a bench
at the Hudson's edge:
rusty and gray
biotite-quartz-feldspar gneiss
a minor marble
stone like sheaves of paper
coming apart in my hands.
I was elsewhere
when my brother died.
How old is the captain?
Flaubert wrote to his
sister Caroline in 1841.
My brother's final breath:
Je vais te donner un problème:
Un navire est en mer…   §

In the Alabama town where I grew up, the town square wasn't a square.

It was round, and it had two Confederate hero statues at one end and plenty of old trees. Grassy patches, where there weren't ant hills, had lots of clover; if one moved fast enough, a yellow jacket could be squashed underfoot. Civil War cannons pointed in all directions. Otherwise there were shops, and the occasional parade, most recently the country's red white and blue bicentennial. The only shop I ever really thought about was the hobby shop that sold electric trains and balsa wood for making airplanes. The owner Mr. Hough, a jolly man in suspenders—whom we were all of the mind might be Santa himself—sometimes traded us a red firecracker for a nickel, and we'd pour out of there into the town square to blow to pieces one of the fire ant hills.

The town square had lanes like spindly legs off in every direction; it was a great granddaddy-long-legs of a town square and down its front right leg there was a hill and a block further down a holly bush that had recently been chock full of spotted grasshoppers, an event that had struck everyone like something out of the Bible. This bush's house with its shutters painted purple was where we had all suffered Mrs. Robertson's kindergarten class.

Our neighborhood was in that same direction on the way to Germania Springs. Germania Springs was where we played tee-ball and flew kites, and where a young aunt of ours practiced her tennis serves with a praying mantis look on her face because she knew she was good, and another young aunt of ours did not drink in front of us kids, and no one understood what drink was doing to her, what it would do, until much later, and no one could see into the future that another aunt of ours would vanish on booze and pills for years, just gone, except she would be heard from, seen, maybe even spoken to, on a rare day, another rare day, and then one day in lower Alabama found dead in her car.

Where I grew up, we lived on West Avenue, though it wasn't west at all, in a house with four front windows—the

sewing room, the front room, a bedroom, another bedroom—
and a Volkswagen bus in the driveway. There were a few steps
up to a front door nobody ever used. It was the side door off
the driveway that put us right in the kitchen where Mom
played games of Scrabble with visitors like Father Tierney.

From the kitchen we cartwheeled into the front room and
then crawled, disappearing from view, under a great tent of
blankets pulled over chairs, the sofa, the desk, held at the
corners with stacked encyclopedias—always surprised when
Mom lifted a corner to look in at what these roly-poly bugs
under their rock were up to.

That was the summer a wailing siren called everyone to
action. Mom swept us down the hall and made us pile in the
bathtub. At the window, her arms pointing into the distance
were like beetle antennae at the glass. She said she could see it,
the funnel, and she told us no, we couldn't go outside, to stay in
the tub, and no, we couldn't have crayons. When the funnel
never touched down, she opened the bathroom door to release
us hopping fluttering somersaulting back into our wild.   §

ON A WINTER WALK, clumps of moss.
How uninteresting.
Why then do I take so many photos?
And hemlock saplings!
Reed grasses
meadow cabbage
and birch, blue cedar, and what not.
Then, the polypody's many little feet,
these wood ferns.
Lichens on bare rock
they say, prepare the way
for a toe-hold.   §

THE ARMORED VEHICLE wakes up in the morning
and doesn't know what it's in for.
It makes coffee, clicks through headlines
of the business section.
The armored vehicle wakes up in the morning
and doesn't stretch.
It used to, a great start-the-day stretch,
with arms up, tipping back,
as if to pull itself off the ground,
as if to say Ready, Set—
It only pisses, then shaves.
Then goes to work. Then comes home.
It is safe, except from itself.
No one with light weaponry
can get at its bejeweled core,
as suggests Saint Teresa d'Ávila.

The armored vehicle does not think
to go to the monastery for the weekend
but it admires the shape of frying eggs
& snow falling outside on 10th street of
New York City. Where, at night,
there's no quiet.

It has points of weakness
like everyone else,
its wheels, its fuel stops.
The armored vehicle does not think
to pray.
It gains weight. It loses weight.

The armored vehicle double parks
and gets no tickets.
It keeps itself clean. Its chrome
and its white shine in the sun.
The traffic cop absolves it
of moving violations.

It bellows along with songs
on its radio
to tune out
other noise in its head.
It wails of hanging from chandeliers
and of one love.

At quieter times,
gurus come over the airwaves
suggesting it ought to love everyone.
And so it tells itself it does,
and that it means no harm:
Who does it harm, after all?
Who says anyone gets hurt?
It is the armored vehicle,
too proud for gurus.   §

NOT THE SCARLET IBIS
of James Hurst,
not in the tree of Christ,
but an ordinary small bird
a finch a sparrow
brown or gray
may stand
or perch, or light, or sit,
or roost in an ordinary tree.
In the third grade,
I discourteously left
Eva Schumacher below
while I climbed a Rose of Sharon
then leaped to a low pecan branch
to stand,
or perch, or light, or sit,
or roost.
In the seventh grade,
I was benumbed in the presence
of certain girls like Vicki Cannon.
Muted by schoolboy crush,
whenever I saw her coming
I jumped into the nearest tree.
There, I looked around,
pretending to make discoveries
among inevitable paths
of branches,
each its own journey.
I pretended she wasn't curiously
birdwatching me.
She bade me come down.
I lowered myself, and having
found a dead fat bug and a bird's feather,
I handed her the feather.
She blushed. Neither of us
were capable of speech.
For all I know,

she has the ordinary feather
of a finch,
forty years later,
among her sacred keepsakes.
I still have the bug.   §

BEFORE HE STARTED UP THE FORKLIFT
in rural Alabama
in the remote star system of a warehouse
of socks, boxers, and women's dainties,
he checked that the shifter was in neutral.

Before he started up the forklift
he read the sticker
on the dash, *I love what I do,*
the company motto.
His manager, a felon,
had stuck it there.

Two into a twelve hour shift
sunlight pooled on concrete
and whiskeyed the wood of pallets.
The place was darker, the further back.

A pendant swung from his keyring:
Budweiser, the garish red
of horror movie blood.

Before he started up the forklift
he said let angels watch over me
in this forklift today.
The way Mom had said it
before starting up the car
when he was a child.
Please let angels watch over me.
Let there be an angel on top.
Let there be an angel out front,
and on the sides,
and at the back.
Let there be an angel underneath.

Before he started up the forklift
he was a boyish thirty-three

very pale
under an Auburn ball cap
the color of wet slate.
He was a cherub a child-man
with red hair a round face
a red beard and blue eyes,
and he was self-harming.

And so the angels came.
Mickey first, hovering above
the cab enclosure
as a canopy of invisible wings
and talons, to protect.
Gabbie strode out front
of the forks
for she was the strongest.
Uri and Ralph patrolled
the sides.
And Jophie sentried
at the back
for she'd been
a shepherd.

He said that ought to do it.
As he started up the forklift
and felt the engine's convulsions
under his feet.   §

MY BABY BROTHER SAID
I am in utter disbelief
because our family
has no words
for anger our anger
the rageful foam on our lips
the trembling
the fists
the mad horses of us
stomp in silent fury
our lungs at immense
internalized pressure
like compressed gas tanks
delivered by big rig
are utterly silent
behind a slow motion
explosion
of booze and pills
distended liver
of nonresponsive
and of death.　§

VESPERS

NOT POLICEMAN
car salesman,
captain of a towboat,
and not an ad man,
gameshow host,
but to name a profession
that could have suited me
better with you,
would it be prosecutor
and defender rolled into one,
as Kafka's letter to his father?
Detached with objectivity,
convivial, and ruthless.
To put you on the stand,
name your disease,
then leave it to the jury.
Not fisherman,
letting out the line,
losing you to the lake.
How about the defender
Atticus Finch,
a restrained nobility,
a principled man
facing an unwinnable war?
Or the doctor of William Carlos Williams
glazing a red wheelbarrow
beside white chickens
to show you your wounds
and mine, to study
your chart, to prognose
your disease? Instead,
I was the forgiving bookie.
I was trail guide with no agency.
A stableman afraid of a horse kick.
A carpenter with no plumb line.
You were the baby Buddha while
I, ignoring the you of you,

was Jesus without a good joke
to teach you and me to be
nothing more, at least,
than who we were.   §

I'LL BUY ANOTHER SCRATCH CARD
is what I'm thinking
at this Second Avenue bodega.
I'll go back in and try
for the mega jackpot
when a small dog, a mixed breed
with beard, pennant tail
and bald spots, an afflicted dog,
crosses on three legs
as if cars aren't everywhere
oh what would it change if I'd won
when a woman with tight curls
wearing church clothes
reaches in the corner garbage
where I've thrown my losing card.
I always lose. I'm a loser.
She pulls out nothing
while the dog arrives, pees,
and walks away,
then she walks away.
I catch up with them
and pretend that we're
together.   §

Friday breakfast

I don't want to write about the sun's rays gloriously shining down from behind clouds. That's happening outside the windows here at the monastery where I've checked in for a few days. I've been coming here to center-prayer the loss of my brother. Snow is in the forecast, and I guess that's why the sky is unbelievable. Sunbeams are shining down from fluffy cotton clouds like a '70s concert poster. How do I interpret this? It's like a message. Yes, the sun's glorious spray of beams is like a telephone call from heaven. I don't want to pick up the ringing phone that is these sunbeams. I know it's my dead brother calling and I'm not ready to talk about any of it. Do I have to take the call? God, it's annoying that you're calling to connect me to him, and it's still the Great Silence at the monastery this morning until half past eight, so please be more courteous about your disturbances. Don't be an ass.

I don't want to write about the family of deer that I saw earlier this morning. They grazed the grassy knoll between the monastery and the Hudson. Then were startled when a brother leaped from the enclosure to his car—they fled, with white tails in the air—as the brother sped away. Why was he in such a rush? The brothers, I imagine, were in need of toilet paper. Or in need of ibuprofen to relieve monastic-wine hangovers. Or air freshener because they'd played cards all night. Hidden away in their enclosure, isn't this what brothers do?

Saturday breakfast

I don't want to write about bees. There are no bees at the monastery, but when there are bees again then brother Aidan will wear the beekeeper hood, taking it from the Prior, brother Bernard, who doesn't want another damn thing on his plate. Brother Aidan also cares for a tuxedo cat named Mouse, who is reclusive and unseen by guests. Now someone has offered to donate a few colonies of bees. In one colony, there may be sixty thousand bees, and a queen. In winter, to stay warm, bees come together, and shiver; all the bees in the hive go round and round in a shivering sphere. Maybe if our own families got together in winter, fewer of us would die. The monastery hasn't had bee colonies for two years. All their bees died because brother Bernard refused any treatments that were not organic—but why? Don't we all know, by now, that poison makes the world go round? Isn't this how my brother saw it, the pill head, the drunk? We are not in a condition, Thomas Merton suggests, to make the best use of our own or the world's goodness.

Yesterday when I heard joyous humming of a Christmas carol, I leaned into the kitchen: the happiest brother I've ever seen, wearing a white apron, flung pizza dough into the air. My brother worked as a short order cook in Rainesville, Alabama, before he worked his final days driving a forklift in a warehouse. If my brother chose a carol to hum as he flipped an egg over easy, I imagine the carol would have been unreal, warped by his poisons. *Jingle bells, shotgun shells, Santa's got a gun....*

Sunday breakfast

What I want to write about is the divine food. At breakfast the brothers offer boiled eggs, which are as cold, wet, and hard as river stones. Homemade strawberry jam is on the table, mostly, only some of it in the jar. The jam spoon is a long sticky tool shaped like an oar, which is not a spoon.

The brothers offer cornflakes served from a glass container like a barrel. There is such a supply of cornflakes, it's as if they have cornflakes delivered by river barge. And jugs of milk, the bovine divine. Certainly, no one goes hungry. The brothers are as round as tree toads.

This morning some brothers wear sandals to the dining room, though outside the windows the snow has begun to fall. When I see their feet—I rejoice! Baby brother, I recall your feet as a child. Your tiny feet were pink; you were a small, delicate child. You had a whole life ahead of you. As you grew older, when you went rural in Alabama, when you worked in kitchens and warehouses, I didn't think you needed the likes of me. Why would you? Why would I need you? If you were here now, I would bring you coffee. I would bring you a boiled egg and set before you the slender salt and pepper shakers. I would make you a slice of toast with strawberry jam, as you enjoyed when you were a child.

If only you were alive. Visit me here, and I will wash your feet. I am so ashamed that I never did this while you were alive.

Sunday night
This afternoon I volunteered to work in the kitchen. My apron was white, and in bold black letters it read, *Keep your rosaries off my ovaries.*   §

LEAFY PLANTLETS
of a hanging spider plant
string puppets
of children
just out of reach
these siblings
they dance together
to the sweet jazz
of a breeze.
They once did, anyway.
It's how they remember
the early days.
Now the youngest
is severed and floats
on a jelly jar of water
at a south window
where he may or may not
survive.   §

WHAT IF YOU'RE STILL ALIVE
and I'm mistaken
you're living a day
you'd love to live
again and over again
laughing at a squirrel
that backflips,
placing rose petals
on centipedes,
breathing in pine
aromas and loam,
walking barefoot
on warm woolen grass
you're a bit sunburned
because the light felt good
what if I'm not alive
as alone as I am
and at night
your chest rises and falls
you're at home
your eyes open
thinking of campfire
light on a canopy
of hickory and elm
and the stars
my god the stars
you're gathering sticks
for the next fire
and the next.   §

To the addicts down the hall
the cancer ward sends regrets
and wristwatches
it's been engraved, they say
a name you could slip into. §

THE SHREWD CAPTAIN
of a Chinese warship
shed the lifeboats
to the horror of his men.
For they were at war:
in the distance,
a red sky at dawn
of artillery fire.
This captain, wise,
who was he, baby brother,
when you left safe harbor
for a horizon haunted by
inevitability of demise?
An old man,
this Imperial Navy captain,
he'd never been sunk.
He shaved every morning,
wore pressed shirts,
and was vegetarian.
Did those sailors go astern
grip the gunwale and gape
as lifeboats
drifted out of reach—
or did they turn
to clean the guns
paying obeisance
to a wide silent sea?
The captain logged deaths
in his journal and doodled
empty diamonds.   §

AFTER YOU DIED little brother
I returned to Mount Cheaha
of our boyhood where I looked
I looked everywhere
but couldn't find what is called
the blind Boy Scout's trail
that wound itself, you would remember,
and wandered and whipped itself
this way and that, a climb a fall,
switchbacks, a sharp cut to a climb,
to a fall, how was it possible that
its trajectory at the heavens
made sense to anyone *this way to
the heavens and God, it couldn't be*
a way without false summits among the pines.
I couldn't understand it then, the trail,
its aim, no one could, and I don't now.
How did a troop of boys make this?
Did they set a blind boy loose
and follow him—
or was it one Scout,
a Scout who closed his eyes
and went, doors slamming behind him,
through woods and webs
let branches whip his face
stumbled into rock outcroppings
bled, lost footing, and fell.
How could I let you
do such a thing alone?   §

COMPLINE

NIGHT, she walks in;
Cymbal-clashing light, her eyes;
I am powerless.   §

LOCATE ME IN A NEW YORK CITY ASHTRAY
the Washington Square fountain
on a night, in a disaster
of unrealities,
inside the fountain
on inner descending steps
I sit for hours
on stonework at
black water's edge
with cigarette butts
bottle caps baggies
ziplocks the size
of an infant's foot
the detritus of drugs.
The park is full of
unreal shadows
that line up like
boards of a pallet.
My baby brother
immersed in unrealities
drove a forklift that
saved his life no more
than I did.   §

FULL MOON
I admire
your scars. §

THE STICK FIGURE
I've drawn into the scene
on this postcard
wishes you were here.
He's like this,
only a few lines,
when you're gone.   §

THE GREAT SILENCE

AT NIGHT the blankets
are upon me.
During the night,
I roll,
they snap their teeth.
These wool blankets
would rather warm the cook
who stood on his feet all day
and will be of service
tomorrow.
A cook hums himself to sleep.
Nessun dorma,
deliqua, oh notte,
when dawn comes, I will win.
These blankets
would rather warm the feet
of the man who splits logs,
who strikes a steel wedge with
the back of a maul,
then carries wood inside
and builds a fire.
These blankets are impatient,
having once warmed the shoulders
of a hunter and gatherer.
They want a new set of problems.
Instead, another night with this loser?
The lamp with the crooked hat
has had to hear about it all day.   §

NO ONE understood
       you
understood
No one listened
       you
listened
No one heard
       you
heard
No one loved
       you
loved.   §

THE HALVES to us
should've been
the wholes
but we never thought
to see who was who
at the time,
the poets, the biologists
of language, the priests
of play and dove
magic tricks: the likes of
Patti Smith, David Bowie,
reading Dostoevsky,
Solzhenitsyn, and Chekhov,
along with James Wright,
Cortazar, Camus, with cathedrals of
Carver, lost happily, with
Allen Ginsberg,
his fury of bliss, his
fright of a far flung
consciousness,
and Ferlinghetti, his
Coney Island of my tribe,
marching ahead of all of us,
with pills and booze,
leading us into the night.   §

DOGS ARE DYING IN OHIO.
When we got back to our friend's house
where the dogs had been alone
we stepped in piss on the kitchen floor
and stepped in shit
on the living room rug
in the dark bowels of her house
with shutters shut and heavy drapes
our friend she leaps from her cave
to take on the world.
Now she cradles an old dog
in her lap. It's dying.
It's her first again.
It's Denver again.
It's Dakota.
It's Dundy.
And we cry with her
for the loss of loved ones
and our own, our own firsts.
Now four dogs are with her
but dogs have worms
dogs have sores
dogs are older than any she's ever had
dogs are too weak to walk
the block, for long,
for dogs, dogs are dying.   §

IN THE CANCER WARD
alone in their rooms
these twelve
the patients
put a knitted hat
on their oxygen tank
and band-aids for eyes and lips,
and name the tank Roger,
Gomez, or Edith.

They twirl their
intravenous tubing
coyly when
flirting with
nurses,
who astonish them,
who love them
enough to linger.

These twelve
the patients
whistle like whales
to other patients
and pass notes
by way of
nurses Malinowski
and Anna the Greek-Aussie,
these notes
are love letters
to themselves, like,
I wuv woo, and,
*I must say
the blue brings out your eyes.*

These ten, then, these nine,
lying under sheets
for as long as they have

at this end of their lives
they've learned
to point and flex their feet
wiggle their toes
even baby toes—
they've learned,
lying in a bed,
how to jump for joy.

They schedule treatments
by the stars
in the night sky
out the window
and by animal care
calendars of cats
tacked above
them. This month's
orange tabby is
on her back too,
batting at a tinsel ball.
Her name, it reads,
is Rudy
and *you can take her home.*

These nine, these eight,
reach for the pen
and cross out yesterday
with a line.
Some days they draw
a lightning bolt,
other days a wave,
or a sine curve, either convex
or concave,
the geometries
of their bliss.   §

AMBULANCE RIDES
The ambulance idles at the curb
all lights off,
up from Roosevelt Avenue
between blocks of buildings
these two paramedics
in the front seats
drink coffee from paper cups
they pour from a thermos
and try on each other's sunglasses
knuckle-roll coins
and fold intravenous tubing
into imaginary pets.

These two, on a recent night shift,
pulled a college kid out from under
an F train—
she'd been seen
for hours in Washington Square
tossing bowling pins up into the air
trying to learn to catch them—
she'd dropped herself
in front of the F
at 14th Street.

A day shift, today,
these two turn up the radio and sing
jazz splashing onto the sidewalk
while they can, between calls,
between summons to aid
the men in cardiac arrest
and the seizing teenage girls,
and last week the woman
who'd stood at a window for days
staring at the wall.
She was parched, soiled,
translucent—

and she fell into their arms, lost,
dead.

These days.
These two laze in their seats
play *I spy or somebody'll die*
or they don't
while they wait for what's next
while the wind outside the truck
whips up cigar wrappers
and lottery slips.

These two,
one of them sleeps,
face on the window,
and snores gentle coughs
while the other pulls watercolors
out from under her seat
and paints round full
wet circles of faces.   §

About the Author

CHRISTOPHER X. SHADE is author of the novel *The Good Mother of Marseille*. His stories, poems, and book reviews have appeared widely. He is also co-founder and co-editor of *Cagibi*, a journal of poetry and prose at cagibilit.com. He teaches poetry and prose writing at The Writers Studio. Raised in the South, he now lives and works in New York City.

Established in 2016, PALOMA PRESS is a San Francisco Bay Area-based independent literary press publishing poetry, prose, and limited edition books. Paloma Press believes in the power of the literary arts, how it can create empathy, bridge divides, change the world. To this end, Paloma has released fundraising chapbooks such as *MARAWI*, in support of relief efforts in the Southern Philippines; and *AFTER IRMA AFTER HARVEY*, in support of hurricane-displaced animals in Texas, Florida and Puerto Rico. As part of the San Francisco Litquake Festival, Paloma proudly curated the wildly successful literary reading, "THREE SHEETS TO THE WIND," and raised money for the Napa Valley Community Disaster Relief Fund. In 2018, the fundraising anthology, *HUMANITY*, was released in support of UNICEF's Emergency Relief campaigns on the borders of the United States and in Syria. palomapress.net

CPSIA information can be obtained
at www.ICGtesting.com
Printed in the USA
LVHW090350060520
655094LV00006B/1757